Victorian Doll Secrets

Text and photography by Mildred Seeley

On the cover:
Three Jumeaux share secrets.

Title page:
A Bru Jne on an articulated wood body, a portrait Jumeau, and Andre Thuillier's A4T Bébé.

Scott Publications

SCOTT PUBLICATIONS
30595 Eight Mile
Livonia, MI 48152-1798

Copyright ©1998
ISBN # 0-916809-97-8
Library of Congress # 98-89034
No. 4990-10-98
PRINTED IN USA

Table of Contents

Page 17

Page 67

Page 73

Thank You

I wish to thank doll collectors who sent their encouragement from all over the United States. Special thanks go to Jo Ann Spencer for the loan of her three dolls and the patterns for teddies, and to Anita Ladensack for the use of her sewing boxes. My thanks to Arlene Seeley who did the stays pattern.

I appreciate the other doll collectors bringing in things and offering suggestions, some of which I could use and others I could not.

Introduction

The mystery of what the dolls wore beneath the costumes is solved with this book. Here, reproduction dollmakers and antique doll collectors get to peek under the costumes to see those marvelous "Victorian Secrets."

Few people get to examine or view the underclothing of the wonderful and great French and German dolls. Yet, the underclothing is as much a part of history as the dolls and costumes. In most circumstances, these dolls—some still in their original clothing—are seen only completely dressed and shielded by glass, either in museums or private collections. It is my contention that the underclothing is as much a part of history as the doll and costume.

My dolls wish to show off their lovely, and sometimes plain or crude, white wear. They will, on occasion, show their bodies. Some dolls prefer only to lift their skirts.

I chose to show only dolls in original costumes with original undies, as I want whatever I document to be authentic—straight from the costumes of 100 to 140 years ago.

The purpose of this photographic record is to reveal what is underneath the costume on antique dolls. This exposure will be helpful in recostuming old dolls and direct reproduction dollmakers on what goes where, how it should look, and from what materials it should be made. (I hope to never again see silk underclothing or colored underclothing on antique reproduction or old dolls.)

So, join me for a study of original doll costumes, from "skin" to dress, with emphasis on the white-on-white underneath. Study also the methods for cleaning, mending, and general preservation of antique doll underclothing.

Mildred Seeley

With one exception, which is marked, all dolls shown in this book belong to the Seeley Collection.

*A Tête Jumeau in her own
elaborately decorated dress.*

Part 1

Underclothing & Antique Dolls in Original Costumes

Andre Thuillier's 21" bébé is one of my choice dolls. She wears a dress and bonnet of aqua-green silk taffeta that is actually a darker shade than I could get it to photograph.

Starting at the dress's neckline, a front panel of tiny stitched darts widen like sun rays until they reach a hipline seam. There, the skirt's pleats begin under a bit of old lace. The shoulders of the faux jacket are edged in lace that extends down to three covered buttons on each side.

The back view shows the stiff cotton dress lining and the lace-trimmed dust ruffle. A metal band on the number one petticoat holds out the skirt so it's full in back.

Under all these layers, she has drawers of an unusual design, with the fabric gathered to a wide top band. Please note each just-below-the-knee leg has a tiny band which allows the lace-trimmed fabric to ruffle. The chemise, shown on the wooden dress form, buttons on both shoulders.

The chemise and drawers are the first layer. Over these, she will wear another full white petticoat trimmed in lace with a pink ribbon threaded through it.

A front view shows off the marvelous detail of the doll's original dress.

The layers of undergarments are shown in this back view.

Note the unusually wide top band on the drawers.

The Schmitt sisters measure 10" and 11".

Note the original tummy sticker on the larger doll.

Here we have two marked Schmitt sisters, purchased fifteen years apart. One sister has brown eyes, the other has blue. Both have the clothing that was made for them when they were created.

The girl in pink still has her tummy sticker identifying the boutique where she was dressed. Her pink shoes are still with her and neither wig nor hair ribbons have been changed.

I feel these little ten- and eleven-inch Schmitts on Schmitts' bodies are worth preserving as long as possible. (Their photograph will be helpful in extending the time.) They are marked 4 and 3/0.

Both costumes, even though they are very different, are couture masterpieces. Each set of fine, lace-trimmed white linen underwear exhibits the very fine stitches and construction of a skilled seamstress. Both wear what we believe are Schmitt shoes—and yes—the old socks.

The dolls' white chemises are pleated down the front and back, and have lace-trimmed armholes and necklines. Their knee-length drawers are linen trimmed with a little lace. Both garments open down the front.

Doll in Red by Etienne Denamur

Can you believe she is just 13" tall? She's marked "E I D." Over the years, there has been much confusion as to who really made the dolls marked E D. Now we believe the maker was Etienne Denamur.

The doll's bisque is absolute perfection and her body, hands and feet are also perfect. It seems she just came off the assembly line.

The satin dress is top-layered with net and lace. There are two layers over the skirt, one short and one full length. The bodice and sleeves are completely covered with the lace. A red silk sash is a slightly lighter shade than the shoulder bow. She has matching red socks.

The bonnet is a most elaborate French style with a high, heart-shaped gathered brim. Matching red ribbons bedeck the high crown.

Under that marvelous gown, our lovely model wears white, commercially-made undies: a chemise, three petticoats, and drawers. All were made of a stiff, white-filled, coarsely woven cotton and edged with the same lace.

The first petticoat should be referred to as the dust ruffle. This is very full and has no top band. Instead the fabric was tacked directly to the skirt.

Originally, it was just long enough to show a tiny lace edge below the dress skirt.

The second petticoat is very full and finished at the top with a band. It is finished on the bottom with the same lace as on the dust ruffle. The third petticoat has very little fullness. It does have a top band and the same lace on the bottom.

Her drawers come to just below the knees and, of course, are finished with the same lace. The chemise is cut rather high around the neck and has lace at both neckline and armholes. The bottom is unfinished.

The underclothing appears to have never been washed and the doll seems not to have been played with.

A perfect E I D made in Paris by Etienne Denamur between 1887 and 1899.

Here you can see the three layers of petticoats

The drawers reveal how the white filling has worn out of the coarsely woven cotton. Note the jointed limbs on the old body.

This close-up shows the quality of the lace that trims all the undergarments.

Nearly every collection of any size will have at least one doll of unknown origin. That is part of the fun of collecting and researching.

This 22" doll is incised with a "C" and either an "F" or a "T," and with an "F" underneath. She is dressed in a most attractive Brittany costume. That French head was pressed into the mold.

Her full, black velvet dress has borders of embroidered design in shades of gold and orange. Between rows of chain and cross-stitches is a band of tiny multi-colored embroidery roses and leaves. This design is repeated in a smaller version on the sleeves and yoke. A small black apron with an embroidered edge tops off the costume.

Over her soft brown mohair wig is a black lace-trimmed cap and over that is a lace bonnet. (I was told that men did the embroidery and women made the lace.)

The style of underclothing does not match the Brittany Wedding Couple that I have had for some twenty years.

She wears lace-trimmed, ankle-length drawers made of a crude muslin bleached white. (The lace is fraying.) These are held up by a drawstring in the top band and tied in the center back—or possibly pulled around and tied in the front.

Her crude chemise looks like it could have belonged to a size larger doll. It is muslin with no decoration. There are two full petticoats; the outer one is an inch or so longer with a crocheted edging.

After undressing hundreds of dolls, one gets a feeling for original clothing and can nearly always identify original or added-to pieces, even if they are old. These are the correct pieces of underclothing for a French doll of about 1885. With study, these pieces, though all made of muslin, still do not quite match.

A French doll by an unknown maker.

A close-up photo shows the face detail. Look closely to see the black trim on the cap hiding under the lace bonnet.

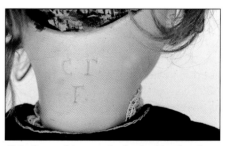

Note the markings on the back of her head.

Note the variety of lace and handwork on the outfit: the unusual lace bonnet, lace at wrists and neckline, and crocheted edging on the petticoat.

Sample of ethnic Brittany-type embroidery borders on apron (top) and dress (bottom).

3/0 Steiner

Here is another experimental Steiner body; see the balls in the joints of her wooden arms and legs. Her face is the very early one with the sharp nose, thin brows, outlined lips and small eyes. Her original papier mâché pate is covered with a skin wig.

The partial label on her back is from her boutique. The remaining letters are:

    (AU NA
    (E CHA
    (Boalldes Cap
    (PARI

The underclothing appears to be commercial and machine sewn—but darling. The split drawers have a tie string and are edged in embroidery and lace. Her chemise has a lace yoke front and back, front gathers, bottom tucks and a lace edging.

The raspberry color French dress is lined and the skirt is fully pleated. Note the beading on the ruffled neckline. Matching ribbons are stitched into the shoulder seams and tie in bows about midway on the sleeves. The bodice seems almost three-dimensional, accentuated by a V-shaped band of black ribbon and a tiny ruffle extending from shoulders to waist. The sleeves end in delicate wrist ruffles.

Her black velvet hat is banded in the dress fabric. A few flowers and some straggly pieces of feather show above the brim.

An early Steiner. Note the unusual joints on the wooden arms.

Two tiny, mint condition Steiners with fantastic jointed wood bodies have metal hands, perhaps of pewter. Both dolls have original cardboard pates and wigs. Look carefully to see the red outlines that remain around their toe and fingernails. Their ears are pierced.

Each is marked on the hip with "Le Petite Parisian, Bébé Steiner." The eight-inch doll with the brunette wig and blue eyes is marked on the back of her head in red: "J. Steiner, J. Bourgoine SFGDG 4%A." Although their bodies and condition are identical, the blonde's head is incised "C."

The dolls are dressed as twins, with handsewn underclothing and dresses. The photograph shows a simple frock of light gray fabric topped with a white pinafore.

These sweet little girls are choice dolls for study and "for keeps."

Note the metal hands and mint condition jointed wood bodies. The waistband and crocheted leg trim on this pair of drawers differs from those worn by the blonde doll.

It is easier to see the simplicity of the outfit in this photograph.

Note shoes, socks and design of this doll's drawers. She has a "C" incised on the back of her head.

Dolls like this one are hard to find, so the only way to preserve them is through photography and reproduction. The E J A's were produced for only a year and made in only two sizes. This 26", all-original example is well worth copying.

Her thick blond wig is topped with a bow of the same silk fabric as the dress, a moss green with tiny, almond-shaped dots the color of straw. The dress silk is deteriorating and faded.

A two-inch ruffle goes all around the shoulders to the back opening. Chenille-like flowers ring the neckline above the ruffle, another version encircles the waist over a teal ribbon belt. From this belt hang three ribbons of dress fabric, each ending with an elaborate decoration of this cream-color chenille. Chenille tabs gather the sleeves at the wrists.

The doll's whitewear is made of heavy cotton. Her chemise has over-the-shoulder straps and a straight body section that buttons in back. The fully gathered, tucked petticoat buttons onto the chemise. Her underdrawers are rather loose with a ruffle and lace at each leg bottom. The top is split at the sides and also buttons onto the chemise.

A front view shows the old dress and matching head bow.

The sleeve tabs are best seen on the back view.

A close-up of the chenille-like decoration at waist and front belt tabs.

The three-piece underwear set. Note buttons at front and sides of waistband.

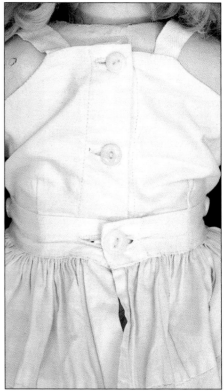

The petticoat buttons to the chemise at the waistband.

The underclothing seen on Jumeau dolls—when original—is very interesting. Its purpose is to shape the doll's outer garment.

Here you see stiff gauzy fabric tucked, then gathered, then gathered some more at the back to attain the bustle-like shape. As if more could possibly be needed, the teddy (one-piece top and drawers) is pulled together at the top with tie strings and the hip section has a drawstring to gather more fabric for the bustle effect.

This Tête Jumeau would have been dressed during or after 1889. We know this because teddies were not used earlier on Jumeaux.

Our Tête Jumeau outfitted in a gauzy fabric, simply and effectively decorated with a lovely braid.

A back view shows her markings and the skirt's exaggerated fullness caused by both its and the undergarments' design.

A very full petticoat, also tied at the waist.

Her teddy with back ties.

Here's a happy trio circa 1912. The 30" and 31" dolls are on wonderful toddler bodies. The 236 Laughing Jumeau was dressed as a boy and wore no underclothes. The 251 wears a white handmade dress embroidered in blue, and drawers, a baby's knit undershirt and a slip. She has on baby shoes and white stockings. Obviously, she's been redressed with loving care.

The 247 wears an old sailor suit that fits her. Her only underclothing is cotton drawers with a touch of lace.

Our trio lines up to show off their unique attributes.

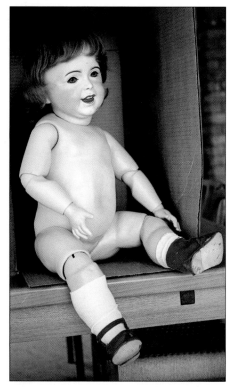

Our Laughing Jumeau shows off his wonderful toddler body.

The trio turns their backs.

Two Jumeaux

The girl is an E.J. and the boy a Tête. Both are in original costume. Ernestine Jumeau dressed him in a costume for an opera that was being presented during the New Orleans Exposition. There are no underclothes.

The E.J. wears white broadcloth underclothing, all decorated with the same lace. The sturdy fabric has held up well through the play years; there is not a thin or torn place in it. The drawers have a band-and-button closing, as does the six-tuck petticoat.

Her couturier-made gown is of deep red velvet as soft as butter. The ivory lace overskirt is matched on the collar and elbow-length sleeves. A large bow and bustle add interest to the back of the dress.

E.J. Jumeau and Tête Jumeau

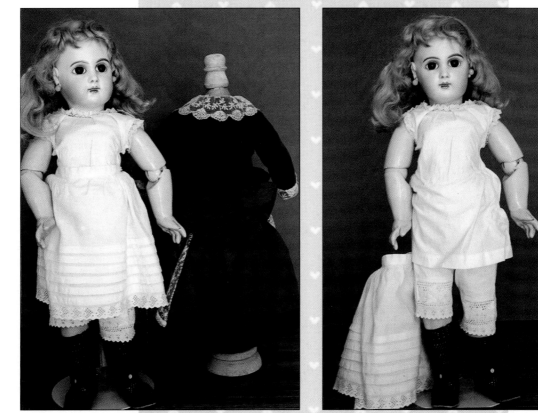

A bow and bustle at the back of the velvet dress.

Her sturdy cotton whitewear has held up well through play and age.

Couturier Costumed Jumeau

Every bit of this 13" Déposé Jumeau's costume is her very own. It is well worth copying. What appears now as a monotone was once a mauve dress overlaid with layers of cream lace. Lace covers much of the front, including the box pleated skirt. Once, her shoes and socks were pink.

Her lace-trimmed drawers of stiffened cotton attach to her chemise. Over this is a full, stiff petticoat and dust ruffle attached to the skirt.

We often find this style of jacket with edges of cording. Cording was also used as designs on the front yoke, belt and sleeves. The original ribbon is still at her neck.

Our little lady wears a completely original costume.

This close-up shows the detail on jacket and bodice.

Tête Jumeau

She still has her earrings, but she's lost her drawers! A commercial white petticoat of stiffened gauze is tied at the waist with string.

Her cornflower blue silk dress has elbow length sleeves. It's covered with tissue silk taffeta and lace; a masterpiece of lace designs and gathers. Extra fullness at the sides and back of the skirt give it a delicate shadow play of lacy patterns. The blue in the ribbons matches her eyes.

This is her very own old gown and an unusual one for a Jumeau. The dress is fast deteriorating and I hope these photographs will inspire some seamstress to make a copy. It will take time and ever-so-much hard work.

A full-length view of this elaborately decorated dress.

A close-up of the dress and hat shows the pattern of overlay of tissue silk taffeta, the lace patterns, and tucking.

Look at My New Dress! Incised Jumeau

Even though this costume does not even resemble an old one, our 22" incised Jumeau is included because of her delicate, handmade white cotton underclothing.

The petticoat is attached to the top, and hand embroidery embellishes the neck, sleeves and ruffled skirt. Her split drawers are edged in nearly two-inches of lace, actually two different laces of the same pattern, one larger than the other, sewn together.

A 22" incised Jumeau wears a new dress.

The rest of the ensemble; handmade underclothes, shoes and socks.

Note the rickrack trim on the petticoat and the lace trim on the drawers. She holds a diamond patterned sock.

What a face! That not-quite-happy baby doll with the puckered brow has no eyebrows and just slightly molded hair of golden tan. Her broad nose and rosebud mouth are finely modeled, and her blue sleep eyes have light gray lashes. This doll is not found very often and even less often with a label intact.

I photographed this doll so you can see the charming (but commercial labeled) christening dress. The dress has only a safety pin closing the back. Her bonnet—an add-on—is a beautifully handmade piece.

Underneath is a cloth body, composition starfish hands, and cloth legs covered with stockings and old booties. She wears a three-corner diaper held with a safety pin.

The garment under the dress is white cotton with scalloped edging and fine hand embroidery. It, too, must have been added.

Tynie Baby wears a sweet, commercially labeled dress and handmade bonnet.

The original label on the dress.

A good look at this remarkable, quite lovely, bonnet.

Under the dress is a garment that has been added to the ensemble.

A good companion for the worried Tynie Baby is this charming laughing baby doll with the so-called open-closed mouth.

The outfit she wears is completely hand sewn, obviously done at the same time by the same person. Look carefully at the row of lace going from neck to wrist, the rows of lace insertion on the bodice, the lace-trimmed scalloped bottom, and the embroidery on the lower skirt. The dress closes at the back with ties.

Her long, white embroidered full slip covers one of wool. This, too, has a scalloped, embroidered edge. Every piece is white-on-white, except for the old pink ribbon on the lace-trimmed bonnet. (If she ever had diapers, she's lost them.)

A happy baby doll from Averill. She wears a hand sewn outfit.

Note all three hemlines, dress, slip and wool underslip, have scalloped edges.

An old pink ribbon on the bonnet is the only color in this white-on-white ensemble

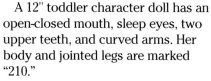

A 12" toddler character doll has an open-closed mouth, sleep eyes, two upper teeth, and curved arms. Her body and jointed legs are marked "210."

She wears matched, original commercial clothing, including white socks and her old cloth shoes. Next to her body is a cute little teddy with pink embroidered scallops around the neck and legs. Over this is a drawstring petticoat with the same decoration.

Her well-designed dress is a soft, cream colored wool challis with four tucks down the front bodice. The skirt is gathered into a waistband of open work threaded with pink ribbon, an embellishment carried on at the neck and sleeves. Some light pink embroidery can be detected along the skirt's hem, directly under the ribbon. An embroidered bonnet covers most of her short baby haircut.

This is a good example of an original German doll outfit, especially the underclothing.

Look closely at the way tucks, open work and threaded ribbon are used in this original German doll outfit.

A close-up shows how this sweet bonnet frames the chubby baby face.

Note the matching scalloped edges on the teddy and petticoat.

An early kicking-crying Steiner, still working, came in a box from Canada. She is in unplayed-with condition and has her own dress and underdress (or slip). Both pieces are trimmed with the same lace and I inserted new ribbon where the old was in shreds.

A lace yoke on the dress comes to a point in both front and back, with ruffled lace around the neck and around the yoke. The bottom of the full skirt is layered. From top to bottom these are: four tucks, lace insertion, five tucks, lace insertion, six tucks, two rows of fine feather stitching, then a wide gathered lace with ribbon.

The main seams are French seams, and everything on the dress is finely sewn and finished. The back fasteners are three fabric-covered buttons held with crocheted loops.

Because of the doll's kicking mechanism, there are no drawers to cover her legs and windup keys.

The entire ensemble, doll and costume, are original.

A look at the underclothes. Only the ribbon has been replaced.

So precious, this Kestner 143 baby belongs to JoAnn Spencer. Usually, we think of baby dolls as only having bent-limbed bodies. But the early babies have the same jointed composition bodies as children dolls.

This baby is lucky to wear all her original clothes. It is apparent some caring grandmother spent months getting this baby ready for the Christmas tree.

Miraculously, that marvelous coat of soft, textured ivory fabric was saved through the years. The wide bertha-type collar and cuffs are trimmed in a special flowered lace.

Her dress is a typical baby dress in batiste with a tucked and lace bodice, and extra lace around the neck. Old pink ribbon still hangs down the front. The full skirt is finished with five rows of lace; the skirt comes to her ankles. The dress has a button closure in back.

Her drawers open down both sides and close with two buttons. They are gathered into a waistband. The legs are encircled with two types of lace. The full petticoat is gathered into a waistband and finishes on the bottom with a ruffle and lace.

The Swiss laces used on all the pieces are matched, except a larger size was used on the dress.

A Kestner 143 with original clothing, topped off by this marvelous old coat.

Her dress shows an abundance of lovely old Swiss laces.

A look at her underclothes and more of the exquisite laces.

Baby Lorie

My kitchen wouldn't be complete without this big Lorie baby sitting in a full-size highchair. All of her clothing, from "skin" out, is the real old baby stuff.

The neck of the yellowed undershirt is scalloped. In addition she wears a short embroidered slip and a tucked, embroidered full slip. Over this is a fine baby gown with homemade crochet on the bottom, down the front bodice and on the sleeves. The choice bonnet has been moved from another doll.

Every morning, Lorie greets me from her highchair.

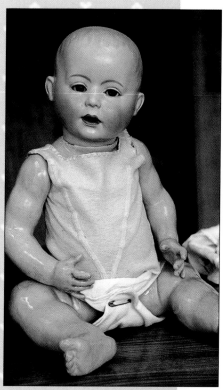

An old yellowed undershirt has an embroidered edging on the neck and armholes.

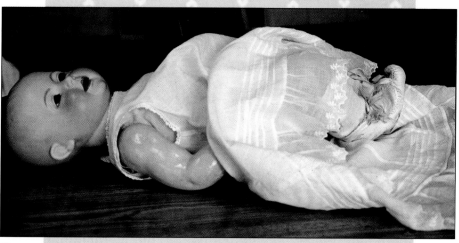

Here you can see the layers of underclothes and those marvelous old shoes.

She is very early French! In most experts' opinions, she is a Premier Jumeau. Her only marking is "O."

All 17" of her is original, starting with her sheepskin wig that still has the original pink ribbons *nailed* just back of the ears. Matching old pink ribbon is still around her neck and on the shoulders of her linen chemise. The lace-trimmed bonnet has the same melting pink ribbons.

The chemise has one tuck and a scalloped edge on the bottom. It ends just at the lower edge of the knee joints. Each leg of her white cotton drawers ends in a border of two tucks and a ruffle. They are held up with a tie string.

Over these pieces she wears a flannel petticoat with a cotton top that buttons up the back. This is topped with a full petticoat of linen, gathered with a tie string and edged in lace.

Her original dress of the finest translucent linen is lavish with lace, tucks and ruffles. The socks are very fine wool, edged in red.

This is a most unusual costume for a French bébé. She gives the impression of being a toddler. Another startling fact about this doll is her baby sister, a French bébé also dressed in white. (See accompanying Portrait Jumeau.)

Most experts grade her as Premier Jumeau.

Back view of the all-original costume.

The first layer under her dress is a linen petticoat tied with string.

The second layer of underclothes is a petticoat of cotton and flannel.

She is not marked, but Florence Theriault says she is a Portrait Jumeau, as is her sister. This is also from an original owner family.

She is, and always has been, dressed as a baby. Note the thin eyebrows and skin wig. There were no curved-limb baby bodies when this doll was made. Her body is the earliest one with joints made of paper mâché.

Her dress and petticoat are handmade. I was so surprised to find her wearing diapers, and she has a highchair.

A close-up view shows the exquisite coloring on the head. Note the original white earrings that dangle from her pierced ears.

The upper part of her dress shows lots of handwork.

The inner most layer is a linen chemise and white cotton drawers. Take a good look at those socks.

The handmade slip is quite lovely.

Diapers were a surprise.

Presented here are three French porcelain dolls marked F.1.G.—each with a different type body. The earliest has a leather body with a bisque shoulder-plate and hands. She is only 9" with a body similar to a Bru Breveté's. Her wig is getting thin, but she still wears a braid and ribbons across the top of her head.

Her three pieces of underwear are the finest quality of lustrous batiste. Drawers, petticoat and chemise were hand sewn with the tiniest stitches and bedecked with delicate ruffled lace. The drawers have a tiny button and buttonhole-stitched closure, as does the full petticoat.

Her dress is a soft olive or swamp green silk. It was made many, many years ago and is melting in places.

Our second F.G. is on a composition body. You may have read about the dolls with pink, green or blue hair. This is one. Note the greenish cast—you didn't expect kelly green, did you—that blends so well with her costume.

She's dressed in a very pale swamp green silk, printed with the tiniest white flowers. The bottom is finished off with a ruffle and lace. A ribbon sash and beads of a darker shade of swamp green complete the outer costume.

Her green silk hat is the same fabric and color as her dress, and edged in a fragile, fine stiff lace.

Her underclothing is so similar to the first doll. It's quite certain that the same person created both sets.

The third doll in the trio is 24" and on a Gesland body. Not many dolls are found on this body. It has a cotton padded metal armature with joints, all covered with a stretch knit fabric. On this doll, the arms and legs from knees down are composition. The doll was photographed with a sketch (possibly for copyright purposes) of the bare armature and the covered armature.

Although these bodies are called Gesland, they were designed by Maillot. According to F. Theimer, it was the patent of Pannier and sold to Gesland to produce.

This lovely F.G. wears heavy cotton split drawers with a pull string tied in back, and a ribbon through the eyelet on the legs. Over this she wears a petticoat with a top, another petticoat over that, and then the dress.

Her white dress of fine, net-like fabric has a two-tier skirt, each ending in a lace-trimmed ruffle. A wide, embroidered lace collar tops off the dress. This is a commercially made, machine stitched dress.

I have a fourth F.G. measuring 24" on an articulated wood body. She has been showing off her wonderful body so long that she has lost her clothes.

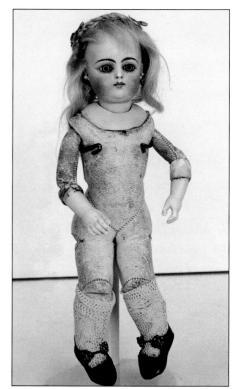

Doll No. 1: Her leather body is very similar to those seen on Bru Brevetés.

Her three-piece set of underwear is made of the finest quality batiste.

A back view shows details of the F.G. underwear. Look closely for the F.1.G incised into her head.

Doll No. 2 has a composition body and a hat with an unusual brim of stiffened lace.

Doll No. 3 wears a commercially made dress of fine, net-like fabric.

This is the full petticoat with a skirt of eyelet.

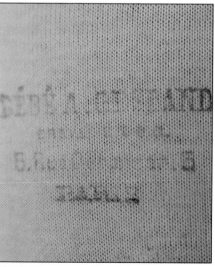

Note all the elements in this picture: the knit fabric "skin" on the body, composition arms and legs, split cotton drawers and black leather shoes.

A document showing a sketch of the metal and covered armature.

The faded stamp on the fabric body covering, establishing the Gesland manufacture.

These precious dolls, marked only with an H and a number, are hard to find and even harder to pay for. They were only made for a short time and only in a limited number. The maker of these luxurious bébés, Aristide Marcellin Halopeau, declared bankruptcy in 1889.

H-dolls, if they have not been changed, are on individually carved wood bodies. This one has her original body and wig, and some of her clothes. The chemise looks like it has never been off the doll, but the drawers seem a little short. They are of the doll's vintage.

I repaired the dress, added ribbon to the hat and front of the dress.

A truly marvelous example of an H-doll.

Vintage drawers may or may not be original to the doll.

The simple chemise is like new.

K & R 109

Our model's regional costume appears to be commercial because it is completely machine stitched. Her drawers are machine sewn, but the added crochet is handmade. The ruffle on the petticoat also was added.

There seems to be considerable variety in the clothing worn by K*R dolls, much of which is quickly and cheaply done. Even the sock tops here are not hemmed.

*K*R 109 in a commercial regional costume.*

Handmade additions have been attached to the original commercial underclothing.

K & R 117

She is all original except for her shoes, which were the painted cloth type worn by so many German dolls. They have completely disintegrated.

Her dress is one I've seen in advertisements. There are only two pieces of underclothing, and the petticoat could be a replacement. It is gathered into buttoned band, and has tucks and a lace edging. The drawers have a band and are open down the back. There is wide lace around the legs.

There is no chemise with this set of underwear.

This same dress has appeared in advertisements.

There is no chemise with this set of underwear.

*A pair of 8", all original K*R dolls.*

She wears a pair of commercially made drawers, held with a drawstring.

Once again, the boy doll has no underwear. The girl doll is dressed in a matching set consisting of cheap, commercial, lace-trimmed drawers with a top tie string, a plain chemise, and drawstring petticoat.

A plain hip-length chemise tops off the drawers.

The three-piece set of underwear includes a petticoat trimmed in matching machine-made lace.

In contrast to the K*R dolls that precede this one (109 and 114), this 112 seems to be well costumed, even though I believe the pieces to be commercially made. Perhaps the larger sizes—she is 22"—were more expensive, therefore costumed better. She wears a full slip, an underpetticoat, and a shirt.

*A large 22" K*R 112.*

This is the first boy doll I found with underpants! Another original costume; the underpants match his kilt.

A 14" K*R 101 wears an original costume.

Underpants match the kilt.

Another K & R 114

I have never undressed this attic-find doll. As best I can see, her underclothing is only stiffened gauze. It seems many German dolls were little more than wrapped and a few stitches added. Possibly the interest at the time was in the regional costuming.

Seemingly, the costuming emphasis at the time was on duplicating ethnic design.

Though commercial, the white-wear under the white dress is very well done. Here we see a teddy— the waist-like top has buttons— and drawers that open and button at the sides. The fabric appears to be batiste, the same as the lovely white dress and bonnet. Her petticoat is very full and opens in the back. There is a ruffled bottom.

A lovely batiste dress and bonnet.

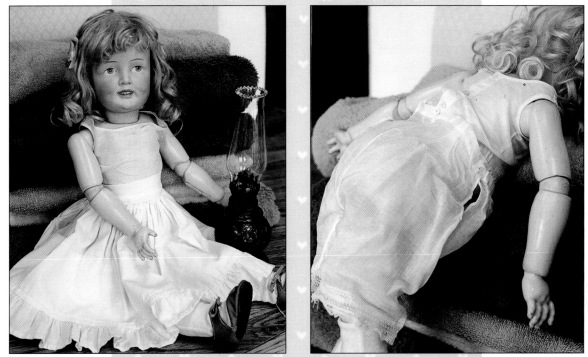

A very full petticoat is the top layer to the underclothing.

A two-piece teddy; the drawers button to the top.

Here are the five characters from Louisa May Alcott's popular book, *Little Women*. The book, movie, and dolls have been recycled, revised, and redone numerous times since their origin in 1880.

These five dolls are the original Simon & Halbig dollhouse dolls. They are marked "S H" and the number "1160." All five are bisque shoulder-plates with open heads, glass eyes and wigs. The plates have breast modeling, but no sew holes.

From the knees down, the legs have various stockings and shoes. *Marmie* wears white shoes with straps and heels. She has only spoon hands, with thumb and fingers together. The painting on this doll is as fine as that of any large doll.

We show *Marmie* in her underclothing. The soil, age color, and the fact it is sewn to the body, leads us to believe it is original. As you can see, it is little more than unhemmed gauze wrapped around the doll's body, an indication of how crude the underwear could be. A cheap commerical "lace" edging rings the hemline and sleeves.

Her gray wig, graced with two tiny ribbon flowers in coral and pale blue, is pulled and twisted into a large knot at the back of the head. It is amazing that this wig has survived the years—as have three of the other little doll's wigs. (I made Amy's, the only one in the set without original hair.)

I have had these dolls for some thirty-five years, having purchased them from their original owner in Atlanta, Georgia. Over the years, not having a dollhouse, I never quite had "the" place for them. Finally, they seem quite at home in my new gazebo.

The five "Little Women" dolls as manufactured by Simon & Halbig.

The underclothing on Marmie, a dollhouse doll, shows the simplicity of design indicative of its origin.

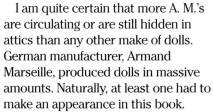

I am quite certain that more A. M.'s are circulating or are still hidden in attics than any other make of dolls. German manufacturer, Armand Marseille, produced dolls in massive amounts. Naturally, at least one had to make an appearance in this book.

I chose this 19-inch A.M. 550 because she's such an interesting character. She was not a cheap doll; her cost equaled that of a very fine Jumeau.

Her underclothing is "mother made." Elastic has been added to the drawers, and the petticoat has had all kinds of adjustments. Perhaps, several dolls wore it before it was her turn. It has not been washed for many years.

The aqua green dress, trimmed in old ecru lace, is charming, worn, and could have belonged to someone else before her—even though she was sold to me as all-original. Her hat decoration matches the dress.

The lovely face of a 19" Armand Marseille 550.

Her dress, obviously old, could have been a hand-me-down.

Her petticoat has had tucks taken across the top, possibly to shorten it to fit this doll.

The elastic added to the waist of the drawers indicates some mother's intervention.

China dolls are judged by hair fashions, facial decorations, and their old bodies and clothing. This one rates a pure ten of ten.

The modeling of her black hair—a fashion of the late 1830s—is very detailed. From a center part, braids are pulled in front of and around her ears, ending in a snail design bun at the back of her head.

Her flesh tone is slightly creamy, her mouth delicate. The two-tone brown eyes have a black lash line and red crease line. She has a double chin. The deep, six hole shoulder-plate rounds downward without much shoulder. The head is hand pressed and without markings.

The outstretched fingers are white and still perfect. Her plain white legs have black flat shoes with red lacings.

At first, because all the fabric was so brown, I thought her clothing and body had been dipped to age it, recalling the French doll reproductions of the 1930s when the leather bodies were dipped to appear aged. Upon close study, though, I decided it was just age or attic color. This fine old doll did not need aging, so perhaps she was left under the eaves or experienced a flood.

All the pieces are muslin, except her two-piece percale dress, which has a little finish left on it. Most, but not all, of the clothing is hand done. Her underclothes consist of a long chemise, below the knee drawers, and two petticoats.

A close-up reveals the detailed hairstyle and the way the lace collar frames her neck and rounded shoulders.

The two-piece, flowered percale dress is of simple design.

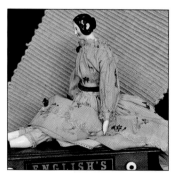

This brown color permeated clothing and body when she came to my house.

A long chemise and outer petticoat are sparingly trimmed in lace.

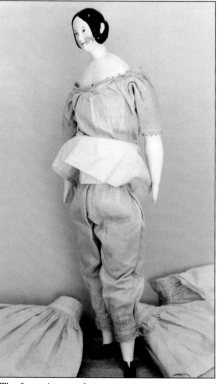

The four-piece underwear set.

Not all French fashion dolls have beautiful underclothing beneath those beautiful gowns. This unmarked 16" fashion has an unjointed leather body, leather arms and separated fingers. What you see on her head is what is left of her wig.

I found the crude, fitted corset interesting. It fits over a simple muslin chemise and a stiff white petticoat with a flounce at the bottom. Behind the doll you can see her two-piece, gray and white striped outfit; both skirt and jacket are trimmed with lace. She has a long, four-inch wide voile scarf for her neck. It, too, is edged in lace.

Take note of the carefully made bonnet. It's quite unique and would make a wonderful piece to copy. Notice that both string ties and wide bands hang from the front sides, and the tucks merge in a point on both sides.

This doll belongs to Jo Ann Spencer.

The ensemble has interesting elements.

A fitted corset of very crude design is most unusual.

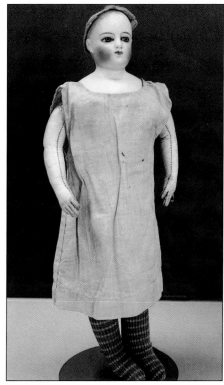

Her chemise is no more than a shift. Note those stockings.

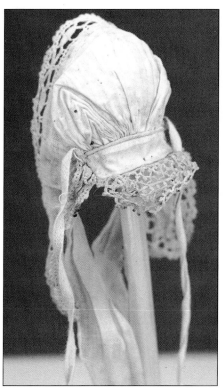

A bonnet worth copying.

Her body and hands are as perfect as any I've seen. And, she has that beloved face. She's all Bru, all 35" of her.

Very few Brus come with their original clothing. This one has borrowed some child's slip and drawers, but look at her Bru dress. It leaves a little to be desired where it's shedding, but there are so few Bru costumes, it should be copied.

I've photographed it front and back so you can see the flowered matte satin. It is a soft cream color with dark mauve rosebuds and moss green stems and leaves. The back panels, sash and sleeves are the same fabric without the rose print.

She stands with two Bru Jne 15 friends. All three have different faces. As I've stated before, one can't judge a Bru by the number. The undressed one is considered a Circle and Dot, but is not marked as such.

The 35" Bru with two friends nearly as tall. Compare their height to the amaryllis, considered a tall indoor plant.

The unmistakable Bru face.

Front view of an authentic Bru dress.

Back view of this elaborate design.

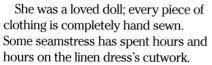

She was a loved doll; every piece of clothing is completely hand sewn. Some seamstress has spent hours and hours on the linen dress's cutwork.

Her linen drawers are split to the band, which buttons in back with a hand sewn buttonhole. There is a ruffle of lace on cuff.

The full chemise, also linen, has sleeves. Below its waist, rows of tucks and gathered lace mirror the design of the long-waisted dress. All of the underwear pieces have matching lace.

A very feminine long-waisted dress of linen.

Note the painstaking detail of this cutwork.

The chemise has sleeves. She wears marked Bru shoes.

Linen split drawers with lace cuffs.

Bru Breveté

She came to me just as you see her—chemise, laced stays, drawers with lace, and two petticoats. She must have had a dress, but this arrangement shows off her all-wood, articulated body.

I hunted all over for this Bru. She was made only between 1880-1882.

Voila! A wooden articulated Bru body.

All three 12" Bru girls, two Bru Jnes and a Circle and Dot, are in original clothing. The one in blue undresses to reveal the underside of her gown, stiffened gauze lining and a full dust ruffle. She had no underclothes.

The other two dolls have full, lace-edged petticoats, chemises and drawers under their satin and lace costumes. All three have leather bodies and perfect bisque hands as seen on the model.

Three 12" Bébé Brus: two Bru Jne, one Circle and Dot.

The underside of the Bru dress shows the stiff lining and how the dust ruffle is attached.

Our model shows off her perfect leather body, socks and shoes.

The 119 is a beautifully decorated doll and so rare I have yet to see her at auction. She's old, on a leather-jointed body, with bisque hands, cloth feet and a bald head.

Her costume of fine translucent linen consists of dress, drawers, a full length chemise, and two billowy petticoats. She looks like a little girl dressed for Sunday school.

The effects of poor preservation and carelessness show up here; the doll resided in the Florida dampness before she came to live with me. I photographed her so that all can see what metal doll stands do—they rust! Note the rust marks on the chemise. Usually, rust marks cannot be removed from fragile fabrics, although treating white muslin with a combination of lemon juice, cream of tartar and sunshine might fade the marks. Simply put, it's easier to prevent than to remove.

The fine points of a very old, rare S&H 119.

Note the rust marks at waist and front of the chemise.

A back view shows the beautifully shaped bald head.

Every time I pass her, she "speaks to me!" When you have a doll that speaks to you after 15 years in residence, you know you have purchased the right doll.

And, since pink is my favorite color, I am particularly fond of her original costume. It is lined with a stiff gauze, with a knife-pleated dual ruffle tacked to that. Her petticoat and chemise were lost through the years, but her tie-string drawers, socks and precious, marked AT shoes are still intact. That bonnet, in the A.T. style with many pink ribbon loops, shows that some seamstress was a master of maneuvering.

A 12" A.T. bébé in original costume.

She wears original drawers, socks and marked shoes.

Study in White
Fabrics Used for Underclothing

Before 1900, doll costumes included underwear made of wool, cotton and linen. These fabrics were made of natural fibers that came from sheep, and cotton and flax plants. I have never found any piece of underclothing—except corset covers—made of silk, even though silk is a natural fiber.

These three fibers produced many grades and types of fabrics. Fine or coarse qualities of thread made the difference in the thickness of a finished fabric. Cloths were determined by the weave itself, and fibers were combined to make something totally different. Many of these variations had names or were made for a particular purpose or group of garments.

Until 1900, white was the color for undergarments. Dolls wore white because that's what people wore. White was easy to wash and iron and, with care, didn't fade or discolor. The natural fabrics were strong, wore forever, resisted tears, and could be decorated with cotton laces, tatting and/or eyelet.

The only colored underclothing were petticoats made of hand loomed wool flannel, which people wore in winter for warmth. There were three colors: natural (cream), bright red and bright blue. I assume children had flannel petticoats for their dolls for the same reason. Dolls wore wool petticoats between the under-petticoat and the full, outer petticoat.

Corsets and children's stays were usually white, although a *very* few ladies wore colored ones.

I couldn't believe how many different fabrics, weaves and mixes of yarns were available to yesterday's doll costumers. Once I started researching for names and descriptions, I couldn't stop. These were all available through numerous magazines, like *Peterson's*, and catalogs, such as Montgomery Ward & Co., dating from 1872.

The fabrics, called "white goods" and obviously all white, were used for drawers, pantaloons, bloomers, waists, corset covers, corsets, petticoats, camisoles, chemises and other pieces of underclothing and nightwear.

Trying to distinguish the fabric in the many, many petticoats and drawers in my collection was most difficult. Some of these fabrics are easy to identify. I found these two tests invaluable: For linen or linen mix, wet a finger in your mouth and place it under a tightly-drawn area of the fabric. If it wets through instantly, it's linen. Satin can be determined by its glossy top surface and dull underside.

Following is a list of fabrics that were sold by the yard under the label "white goods:"

Art linen—pure white, proper weight fabric for embroidery.

Batiste—fine, soft fabric in a plain weave.

Birdseye diaper cloth—durable, absorbent.

Bleached sheeting—strong, evenly woven, long wearing.

Bloomer charmeuse—soft satin weave with dull back, lustrous face; especially suited for bloomers, petticoats and other undergarments.

Broadcloth—originally defined high quality, close weave all wool. Fine, durable, light to medium weight cotton.

Cambrics—lightweight, plain weave linen or cotton; pure white Irish handkerchief linen.

Cheesecloth—open weave; gauze.

Chinchilla cloaking—close knit cotton back; desirable for children's wear.

Dimity—white on white checked design.

Dotted swiss—sheer fabric with white, firmly woven dots.

Eiderdown—knit back, downy mixed face; suitable for baby coats, etc.

Flannel—desirable for petticoats and nightgowns. *Outing flannel*—soft, napped on both sides. *Cream flannel*—woven of new wool and cotton yarns. *Cream all-wool flannel*—pure wool yarns. *Diaper flannel*—good quality bleached. *Baby flannel*—for baby clothing. *White Shaker flannel*—Fleeced on both sides; soft, downy.

Linene—cotton fabric finished to look like linen.

Longcloth—plain white fabric similar to muslin, but lighter and softer.

Mohair—mohair filling and fine cotton warp.

Muslin—bleached, inexpensive, serviceable; desirable for underwear.

Nainsook—fine, soft fabric of combed cotton; slightly coarser than batiste.

Organdy—imported Swiss made of long staple cotton with a permanent crisp finish; transparent.

Pique—light to heavy weight cotton with woven, raised design.

Percaline—firm weave; used for linings, children's bloomers.

Plisse—permanently crinkled; ideal for petticoats or nightgowns.

Poplin—mercerized cotton yarns; fine, plain weave; suitable for children's underwear.

Sateen—smooth, firmly woven, soft, lustrous finish for petticoats and bloomers.

Voile—lightweight, soft, evenly woven.

The spinning wheel was used for making wool thread.

The flax wheel used for making linen thread.

Clark's made and sold thread.

Trims for doll underclothing varies from the very finest to raw material cut with a die or stamp.

A good example of the poorest fabric and trim can be found on Simon & Halbig's "Little Women," dollhouse dolls from the 1880s. The finest lace was used on the Jumeau costumes supervised by Ernestine Jumeau.

Between these two extremes were many types and many grades. Much of the German lace on undies did not survive even one child's laundering. Most of the underclothes that have stood the test of 100 years or more were handmade by a family member of used fabric in good condition. It was decorated with lace, tatting or crochet, or with laces salvaged from family clothing.

As you study doll clothing, you will be aware that it is made up of bits and pieces of all types of materials.

Needle drawers salvaged from an old store.

Tatted lace decorates petticoat and drawers.

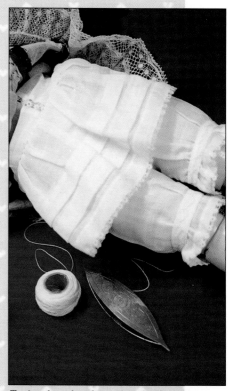

Tatting thread and a tatting shuttle.

Examples of edgings and trims
used to decorate doll petticoats.

Examples of edgings and trims
used to decorate doll petticoats

Antique laces marked Switzerland and France.

Embroidery hoop, folding scissors and an example of hand embroidery.

Buttonhole scissors, antique letter stencils and antique letters to overcast.

Switching Clothes

I call on all doll collectors who are not guilty—not even once—of switching clothing to please stand up! Even dolls exhibited at U.F.D.C. have pieces of clothing added, exchanged, or concocted to make them more presentable. All exhibitors do it to a certain extent, but few admit to the practice. I, too, am guilty.

In one instance, I challenged a group when I could pinpoint examples: changes had been made in clothing, wigs, and one had changed a body. Each person had committed a great sin, but weren't admitting it.

There are things hobbyist doll collectors are allowed to do to improve the dolls to make them presentable in our homes and displays. Oftentimes, hobby doll collectors have two choices: fix and clean the doll or stash it out of sight in its present condition.

In my opinion, we need to face the truth and admit what has been done. After all, these collectors bought and paid for the dolls.

How about dealers? We know—and it's not difficult to see—where one bonnet or shoes were moved from one doll to another to get a better price. It certainly isn't a secret that auction personnel move "stuff" to get a higher price. They also mend and replace.

This whole switching thing is no great sin for the hobby collector, the dealer, or the auction staff. Museums are another matter.

There are times when we do get a doll fully costumed and shod from a first or second generation owner. Such dolls are rare, and oftentimes less expensive than dealer or auction dolls. These are the dolls that should be put behind glass and kept as they are, at least as nearly so as possible.

I'm lucky to have a few dolls of this type to use in this book. Photography is the best way of preserving them. Most have been cleaned and some, but not all, underclothing washed. There are dolls under glass domes that have not been touched in many decades (there are a few advantages to being old).

Underwear Switching

It was very obvious when I was working on the book about china dolls that much of their underclothing had not been made for the doll that wore it. The signs were visible in many ways: overlapping of petticoat bands, skirt bands extended with common pins or safety pins, dress lengths varied, blouses failed to button, and so on.

It is so easy to forget that these were playthings. Doll heads got broken, clothing was stripped and placed in trunks to be used later to dress other dolls.

So, my advice is to make the dolls as lovely as possible and don't hesitate to admit the fact. It's your doll, your money, your time, and all for your collection. However, if you are lucky enough to find or have an unplayed-with doll, save it as an artifact.

Dolls' underclothes are closed in interesting, funny and ingenious ways. These garments—petticoats, drawers and chemises—often made from fine white linen of nearly gossamer weight were usually hand sewn with French seams. The usual closures on these drawers and petticoats were handmade buttonholes and tiny pearl buttons.

Both drawers and petticoats were gathered into neat bands, and the bottoms were finished with a touch of the finest gossamer lace. Smaller versions of matching lace edged necklines and armholes.

Some seamstresses spent untold hours on these projects; less expensive dolls had their commercial, unhemmed underclothes sewn directly on them.

Some of the closures we see today are improvisations by children and mothers who moved the long-lasting underclothes from one doll to another or from attic to doll, using quick methods to make the pieces fit. I photographed them as they came.

A Nursing Bru wears original, tied diaper cloth pants, and a matching buttoned and tied jacket.

Tape goes through the top hem, pulls up, goes around the body and ties in front.

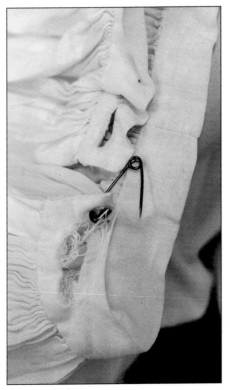

A common pin.

Buttons and buttonholes

Hooks and thread/string eyes.

Ribbon ties.

Old snap hook.

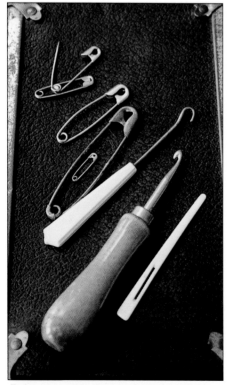

Early commercial safety pins, buttonhooks, and bone for putting in ribbon or tape.

Stitches instead of pins, buttons, etc.

Drawers with elastic (after 1915).

Underclothing Vocabulary

People wear clothing for numerous reasons: tradition, modesty, protection, warmth, beauty, as well as for shaping the body or costume, for activity, health reasons or just habit.

Most of these reasons had little to do with why antique dolls had a plentiful assortment of underclothes. Dolls had underclothing because people did; doll costumers copied human clothing. Often doll clothing was a teaching tool for children, as well as playthings that mimicked real life.

Articles of clothing and the names of pieces have changed over time. In many instances, garments' shapes have also changed. The following list is from old catalogs, ladies' books, *Peterson's Magazine* from the 1800s, etc. I'm sure I didn't get them all.

I have given definitions and as best I could, matched the names with photographs of actual items or supporting illustrations.

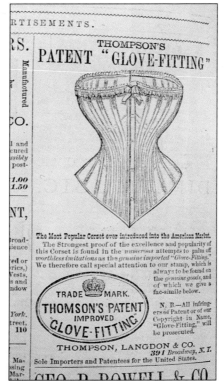

Corset — A stiff, laced affair to improve the figure. An illustration of a lady's corset from Peterson's Magazine.

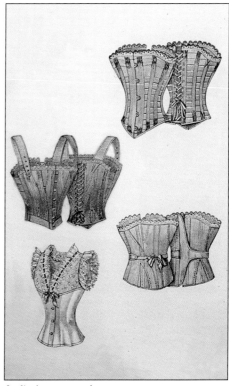

Ladies' corsets and stays.

Vocabulary

Brassiere — Guimpe with long sleeves.
Corset — Stiff, laced affair to improve the figure.
Drawers — Straight legged underpants.
Dust ruffle — Balayeuse—removable ruffle around bottom of skirt.
Guimpe — Top worn under low-necked dress.
Hoop petticoat — Hoops of cane or wire without fabric.
Leglets — Early, used instead of drawers—just legs.
Pantalets — Same as pantaloons.
Panties — Short pants with elastic (1920).
Petticoat — Undershirt.
Petties — Petticoats.
Pinning blanket — Long baby petticoat slit down the front.
Promenette — Corset for child learning to walk.
Sacque — Infant's long chemise.
Slip — One piece top and bottom (bodice & petticoat).
Stays — Corset like for children with straps or ribbon over the shoulders.
Teddy — Combination drawers and bodice.
Umbrella petticoat — Deep ruffled flounce around the bottom.
Union Suit — One piece to cover body of knit material.
Wrapper — Similar to a pinning blanket.

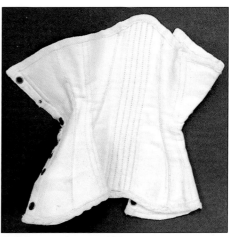

A doll corset from an A.T.

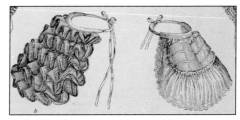

Ladies' bustles.

Underclothing Vocabulary

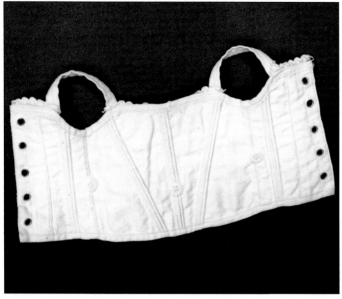

Stays — Corset-like for children with straps or ribbon over the shoulders. These belonged to a Bru Breveté.

Assorted petticoats.

Hoops, corsets, bustle, socks, etc.

Drawers, union suit, one-piece teddy.

Flannel petticoats.

Nightgown.

Bru socks.

Baby pants.

Two-piece teddy.

A Googly shows off her matching dress and underclothes.

Back view of Googly's drawstring drawers.

Recognizing the underclothing worn by the antique dolls is vitally important. The garments must be correct for the doll's age; both in fabric and to enhance the gown that covers it.

During the undressing of hundreds of French and German dolls made between the years 1870 and 1895, I've concluded that the underclothes consist of three essential pieces: chemise, petticoat and drawers.

Most of the dolls wore some type of additional undergarments, such as a corset, corset cover or waist, extra petticoat and flannel petticoat. All of these garments were white, except the wool flannel petticoats which were made in red, bright blue and natural. The whites were made of fine linen, very fine cottons and, occasionally, muslin.

Chemise: Usually completely without shape, and made of two pieces of fabric, front and back alike. There is a short extension over the shoulders, necklines were cut boat-shape and low, so it wouldn't show above the dress neckline.

Most chemises had no closure, just pull strings. Others had shoulder buttons and buttonholes. The neck and armholes were trimmed with lace or tatting.

There were some fashioned with more shape that extended to the neck and closed a simple bound split with ties or buttons. Some, not many, chemises had set-in short sleeves.

Drawers: Most doll drawers were made like those worn by the children of the day. The legs varied in length from boot top to kneecap. Some of the straight-leg drawers were decorated with many tucks, and inset lace that ended with more lace.

Other leg styles had a band at the bottom with little or no gathering. This band was oftentimes embroidered or ended with a flounce and lace.

Drawers called "picnic drawers" were split with no crotch seam. These had no tucks from the waist for fitting and, usually, the tops were finished with a band through which a tape was threaded. This tape came out the back and was pulled around to tie in front.

Another type was gathered into the waistband, and buttoned on both sides; some buttoned in the back only. These were finished on the bottoms with tucks and lace.

Petticoats: Made primarily to enhance the outside garment, petticoats would be just full and long enough to fulfill that purpose. They were gathered onto a band at the waist and fastened like the drawers, with one or two buttons or drawstring.

Some were fixed so only the back was gathered and tied, while others had an extra drawstring across the bustle area to make the back pouf out.

Petticoat bottoms were finished many ways; with countless hand sewn tucks or an added on ruffled or pleated flounce. Most petticoats had lace and some were hand embroidered.

The flounce or lace should not be confused with a lace dust ruffle that shows just below the dolls' skirt. Dust ruffles were attached (tacked) directly to the skirt.

In general: I have found that dolls wearing original clothing have underclothes that match, both the fabric and the lace. Although the lace may have the same pattern, it can be several widths.

There are always variations and some odd arrangements in doll underclothes. Once in a great while, we find a union suit (teddy), a one-piece garment or a combination of chemise and drawers. Most of these came after 1895.

A Steiner's "whites" match in fabric and trim.

She shows off her corset worn over the drawers and chemise with sleeves.

The drawers close with a tape wrapped around the torso and tied in front.

After undressing hundreds of German dolls in search of fine or unusual undies, I became disappointed. The original underclothes that have lasted were found on unplayed with dolls. I found it to be made of stiff mesh gauze, and mostly without design or character. Obviously, these items could not have been washed or even removed from the dolls in one piece.

So, German dolls that had good undies were fortunate to have home-made underwear. The Simon & Halbig 119 was dressed in fine linen, hand-made undergarments; however, many of the play dolls were purchased with cheap flimsy dresses and gauze underwear or without any clothing. Most dolls had just two pieces of underwear: drawers and a petticoat. Very few unusual articles of clothing have been found.

I did find some interesting "mother-made" teddies or combination drawers and chemises. Most pieces were made of muslin or heavy cotton; all were white.

Twice, I found petticoats that button on the top over the drawers. I found both cotton flannel and wool flannel petticoats and some of these had decorative stitching around the bottom. A few of the petticoats had tucks and lace.

I found all kinds of poor machine stitching and poor or child-sewn seams, and a few pieces with superior stitches. Generally speaking, the German dolls were made for families of modest income, while the French bébés were made for the rich little girls of Paris.

The underclothing for the German dolls was factory produced and that of the French dolls was couturier designed along with the costume.

Example of the crude state of German doll underwear.

A Steiner sews dolly clothes on a miniature sewing machine.

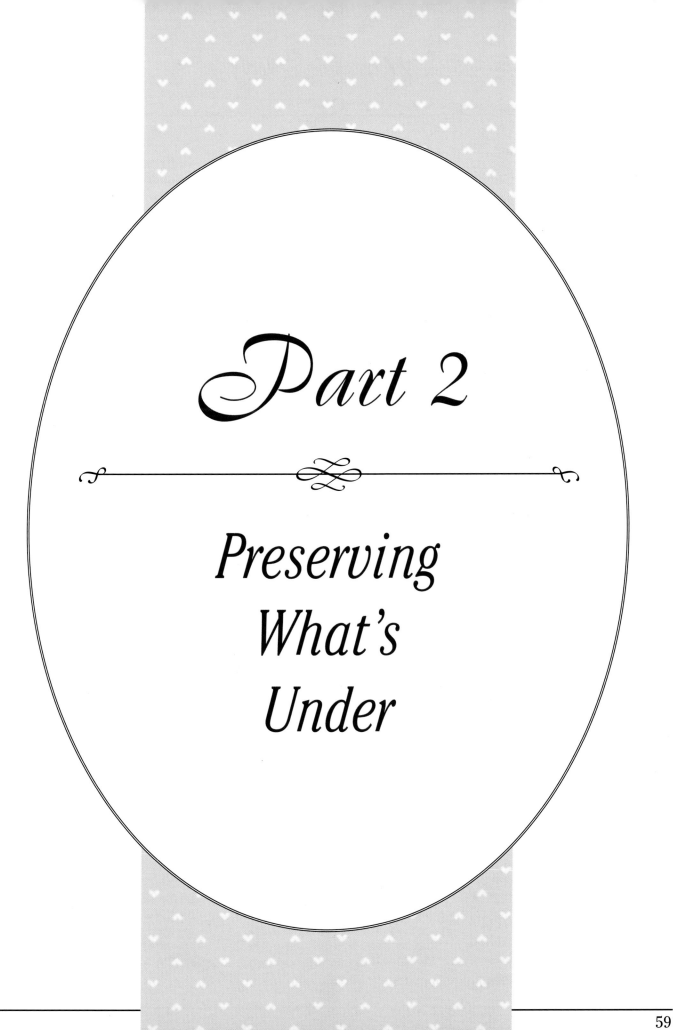

Part 2

Preserving What's Under

Wash Day

This is the way we wash our clothes

Wash our clothes, wash our clothes

This is the way we wash our clothes

So early on Monday morning. &

Washday Before Electricity

At the time the dolls we profile were made and sold, young dolly mothers learned to care for the garments belonging to their dolls by watching and helping with the process, then by duplicating as closely as possible with their toys.

Certainly, we wouldn't use the same methods today on fine linens or cottons. Still, it is good to know just what treatment these garments have survived.

Laundry Day

I remember clearly how laundry was done when I was a child. It took all day—two days when ironing is counted. Laundry day went like this:

Water was pumped by hand outside the back door. A boiler—a large elongated tub about 16" high—was set on the front of the wood stove. Extra wood was piled by the stove to keep the fire very hot. The tub was filled about three-quarters full with cold water and a cup of washing fluid (probably bleach) was added to the water. (My mother made the washing fluid and put it in big bottles to use for six months or so.)

Slivered, homemade soap was added next. (I recall watching my mother line the wooden box with old sheeting and pour hot soap into the box. Before the soap cooled completely, she cut it with a big knife like fudge, only in 6" x 4" pieces.)

The laundry was sorted into three piles: white clothing, light colors, and work clothes. The white wash—sheets, towels, underclothes and handkerchiefs—was added to the still cold water. The lid was placed on the tub and left to boil for thirty minutes or so. (I don't know if this was to get the clothes clean or to kill the germs.)

While the whites boiled, Mother put the light-colored clothes to soak in the hand-turned washer filled with warm water and soap. (The night before, a reservoir of water was put into a tank made on the right-hand end of the wood stove and was ready to use.)

Then she made the starch (Hubinger Bros. Elastic Starch), which she cooked on the stove. Two metal tubs were filled with rinse water. Bluing (Sawyers Crystal Blue) was added to one tub.

After turning the washer for ten minutes or so, the wash was removed, one piece at a time, and put through the wringer (two rubber rollers with a handle for turning). The wringer would fasten only onto the washer, so the clothes were rinsed in clear water, then blued water, then taken to the wringer. From the wringer they fell into a large wicker basket. Anything needing starch was starched, then all were hung outdoors on the clothesline.

By this time, the white wash had boiled enough. Piece by piece, it was lifted out of the boiler water with a clothes stick (a 3-inch stick used only for this purpose), poled into a large pan and carried to the washer. The washer was cranked again, the white wash rinsed, blued, and hung to dry. (Some doilies and napkins had to be starched before hanging.)

While the sheets were being hung, the work clothes were soaking (but not boiled) in the warm soapy water in the boiler. As they were removed to be placed in the washer, they were inspected for spots. These got extra attention with a bar of soap on the washboard. Once washed and twice-rinsed, the dark work clothes were hung to dry on the clothesline.

Clotheslines were made of special glazed rope. The line had to be taken down after every washday or washed off before clothes were hung. Two kinds of wooden clothespins were used, a pinch type on work clothes and the straight pin with two legs that worked best for sheets and towels.

Clothes were hung just so: one pin held the corner of a sheet and the corner of the next piece. This saved room on the clothesline.

Once all the clothes were hung, all the water had to be bailed out and poured in the garden. After the floor was mopped, the laundress was done until the clothes were dry. Then things had to be folded and put away, except what needed ironing.

If the weather was such that Monday was washday, then ironing was done on Tuesday. Early in the morning, the clothes to be ironed were sorted and piled on the table to be sprinkled (sprinkling dampened the fabric so ironing was easy—no steam irons!). A bowl of warm water and fingers were the sprinkler system.

The clothes pile was layered, the top piece was sprinkled, rolled, and so on down. Like pieces were rolled into a towel and the towel was dampened.

The three-cornered irons were put on the wood stove to heat, three at a time. A well-padded board was put across the end of the table, one iron was lifted from the stove, tested for heat by touching with a wet finger, and run over a little bee's wax, then wiped clean by running over an old piece of sheeting. The ironing begins.

A hot iron, handle held with a pot holder, might last all through the first garment, then a fresh hot iron would be used while the first one was put back on the stove to reheat, and so on. Ironing needed to be finished before dusk because the kerosene lamps didn't provide enough light. And so it went, down through the never ending pile of clothes.

I clearly remember when Mother got an electric Easy Washer, and an electric iron which ran on a Delco plant. This was the engine and row of batteries that furnished us with electricity for lighting. (She also got a pulley clothesline, so she could hang clothes from the back porch.)

As children, we mimicked each of these procedures with our miniature tubs and irons, putting our dolls and doll clothing through the entire routine.

Washday, with all the supplies.

Hanging clothes to dry in the sun.

A day of ironing.

Paraphernalia for washing and ironing before households had electricity.

Preserving What's Under

In our house sewing and mending were two different things. Sewing was making new garments, usually for the women and girls, including the girl dolls.

Most patterns were purchased. After all, this was the 1920s. Patterns were packaged in envelopes very much as they are now. We traveled about fifty miles to Oneonta, New York, where we (Mother) studied the patterns on the second floor of Brasees Department Store.

Besides patterns, we might buy braid or binding, nothing else. Dad's country store had bolts of cotton fabric and a few finer fabrics. Mother selected the fabrics for the store, either from a Butler Brothers catalog or during our spring and fall visits to Butler Brothers store, a wholesale place in New York City.

Mother had to plan ahead so she could get a couple of afternoons free of interruptions for dressmaking. She had to bake ahead and plan the meals for a couple of days. My middle sister and I were always in need of dresses, and so was at least one of my dolls.

The dining room table became the layout place for cutting fabric. The Singer treadle sewing machine was housed in the dining room. Mother had everything to work with; Dad's store had cabinets with marked drawers that held thread of every color. A smaller cabinet with two drawers held all kinds of needles. (I have these cabinets in my home now.)

If the dress and matching bloomers in progress were for me, I was encouraged to help with each step.

Clark's cabinet and assorted J.P. Coats threads.

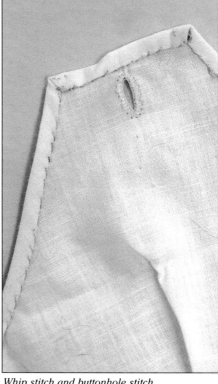

Whip stitch and buttonhole stitch.

French seam.

Herringbone stitch.

Sewing Teaching Aids

It appears that for more than 150 years, sewing boxes and embroidery boxes have been teaching aids for children. Intriguing to look at, these boxes, some used and some never used, now can be purchased occasionally at auctions. They make interesting additions to a doll collection. They become even more interesting when they contain bits and pieces of children's stitches.

Here are three, all undated. As well, I've included pictures of two booklets written in French that were used to help children learn.

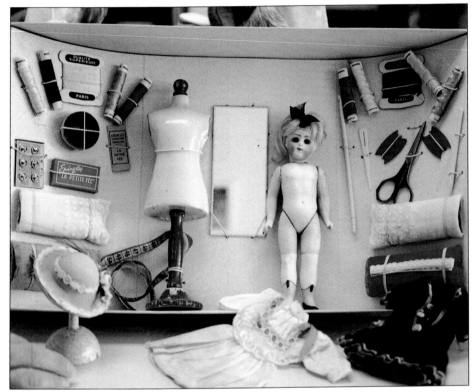

Two types of a child's sewing kit (above and top left).

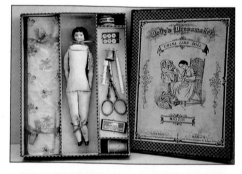

Another child's sewing kit.

A child's embroidery and sewing box (above and middle right).

Two booklet covers from an embroidery kit.

Treasures in Trunks, Boxes and Valises

Pearlized Metal Trunk

Best friends, *AT3 Silver* and *A4T Nanette* share the clothing from *Nanette's* trunk. The dome trunk, 11" x 16" x 10", is decorated with metal treated to look like mother-of-pearl. There is a wide band of this metal across the top, more down the front and on the ends of this very fashionable trunk. The top and sides are reinforced with wood slats.

The inside has bright blue and red paper linings, ladies' photographs on the hat compartment, and a covered division on the tray.

The trunk contains an old faded Christmas card that came with the doll and trunk in 1883 and a newspaper clipping announcing the A4T as a Jumeau. In addition, there's the story of the doll's two owners, Edith Snyder and Agnes Parcel, and how she, the doll, resided in a safe deposit box for 20 years.

Clothing found in the trunk consists of: two white batiste dresses with lace, tucks, and ruffles; one red dress with large puffed sleeves; one blue dress; and another white dress with tiny print in pin and green. There were also three pairs of drawers, five petticoats, two chemises, three pairs of socks, and two pairs of shoes, one marked A4T.

Best Friends

The trunk and clothing belonged to A4T as she came in it from Paris. Because the two dolls, AT3 *Silver* and A4T *Nanette*, came from the factory undressed, they shared the clothing in the trunk. (*Silver* may have come naked, but she had a wonderful story.)

She was the last "belonging" of Baby Doe Taber's daughter, Lillie Taber of Leadville, Colorado. The Tabers were owners of the famous Leadville silver mines of Colorado. Both dolls are dated 1883, 1884, and their costumes, especially the underclothes, reflect this period.

Thuiller dolls share
a trunk and clothing.

A look inside the trunk, decorated with pictures of ladies wearing hats.

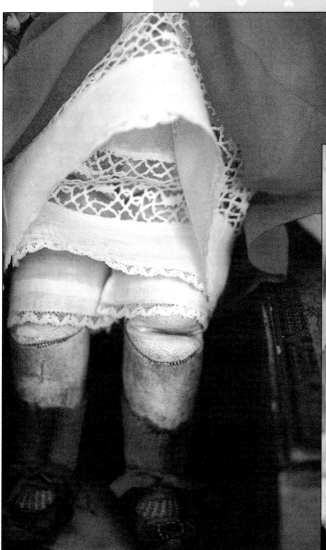

White underclothes on A4T.

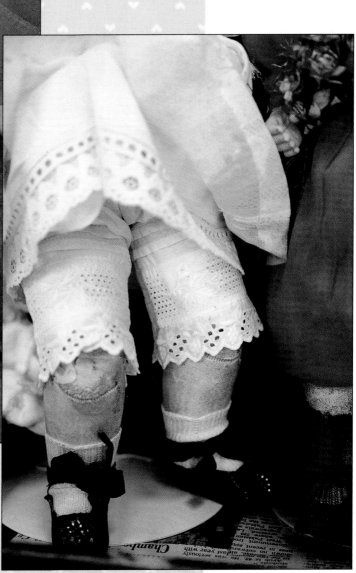

AT3 shows off her white underwear of a similar, but still unique, set of underclothes.

The metal dome trunk was highly fashionable in its time; circa 1883.

Perfection in a Battered Box

This choice, unmarked doll just never got to see the world. If the cover had ever been lifted, her costume would have been faded.

Her underclothing was done by a couturier who also did the costume. It is quite complete.

Her carefully made, short-sleeved batiste chemise extends to her knees. Over the chemise is a short, poorly made corset with four eyelets that lace up the back. Underneath she has drawers with eyelet and tucks that come to the lower calf. A simple but pretty petticoat covers all.

All still together, lady doll, clothing and original box.

How she is dressed directly under the couturier outfit.

How the corset laces up the back.

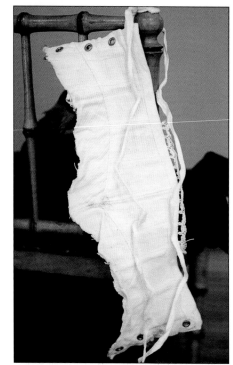

The corset; poor craftsmanship is evident.

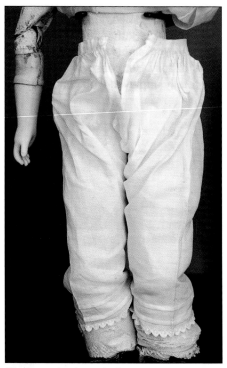

The long, simply made drawers.

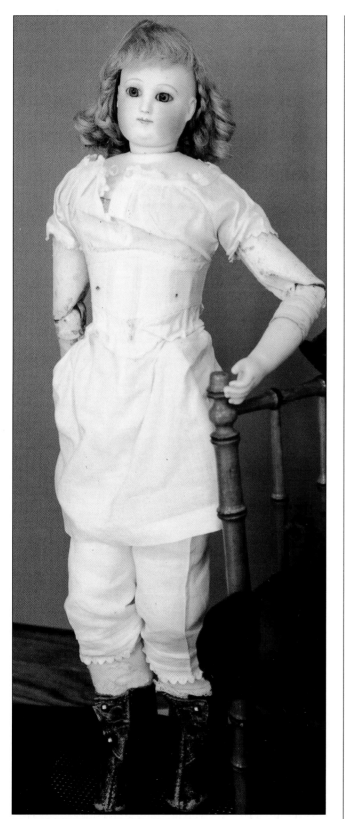

The long chemise covered by the corset.

The Wooden Trunk

According to Jeanne Palen's Scotland relatives, this trunk came to Prince Edward Island, then to New Kingston, New York, in about 1850.

Jeanne Roberston Palen was my childhood playmate, and is still my dear telephone and corresponding friend.

Originally, the trunk belonged to J. Oscar Russel, a brother of Jeanne's grand-father, Andrew Russel. It was handed down through numerous relatives to Jeanne, with the doll still in it. When Jeanne took posses-sion, the trunk (we would call it a wooden chest) had acquired many coats of paint in various colors. Jeanne's hus-band removed the paint and refinished it to its former glory.

The old wooden chest and a Delhi coverlet, dated 1838, has the name Sarah Cummings woven in one corner.

The china doll that lived in the trunk.

Simon & Halbig All-Bisque Bébé in a Box

If we hadn't found her in unplayed-with condition, still tied in the marked box, we wouldn't know for sure that this little German all-bisque was made for the French trade. The label tells us she was dressed in Paris by Au Nain Bleu.

She still wears that stiffened gauze underclothing so, apparently, the dolls were shipped from Germany in their underwear to be costumed in the French manner, then boxed and sold as French. These same black stocking girl dolls were sold in Germany and in the U.S., usually undressed.

The doll, costume and box.

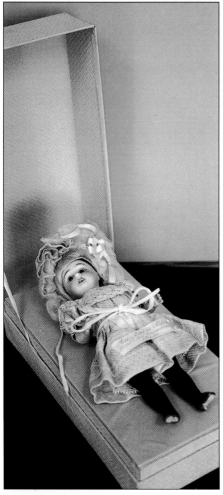

All original S&H doll tied in her box.

The label reveals the origins of the dress.

The crude gauze underwear that must have originated with the doll.

Bébé Jumeau 5

When I found this little Jumeau at a doll sale, she was in her box, marked five.

The commercial chemise, without showing any signs of fading, is trimmed in red. Her shoes are marked Jumeau and her red socks have white detail.

The underwear is made of fine cotton, not the starched gauze we often see on the dolls. The commercial drawers have a drawstring that opens the back, then is brought to the front for easy tying. Cuffs and lace decorate the leg bottoms. An under-chemise is tucked into her drawers.

The petticoat is something of a mystery, as it has initials embroidered on the band. It looks as if it were made with the drawers and under-chemise.

The under-chemise and cuffed drawers.

The Jumeau as she came to me accompanied by her original box.

The "mystery petticoat" has embroidered initials, an unusual and unexplained occurrence.

*A Bru doll with original
clothing shows her stay
with buttons to fasten
her drawers.*

Part 4

Patterns
&
Projects

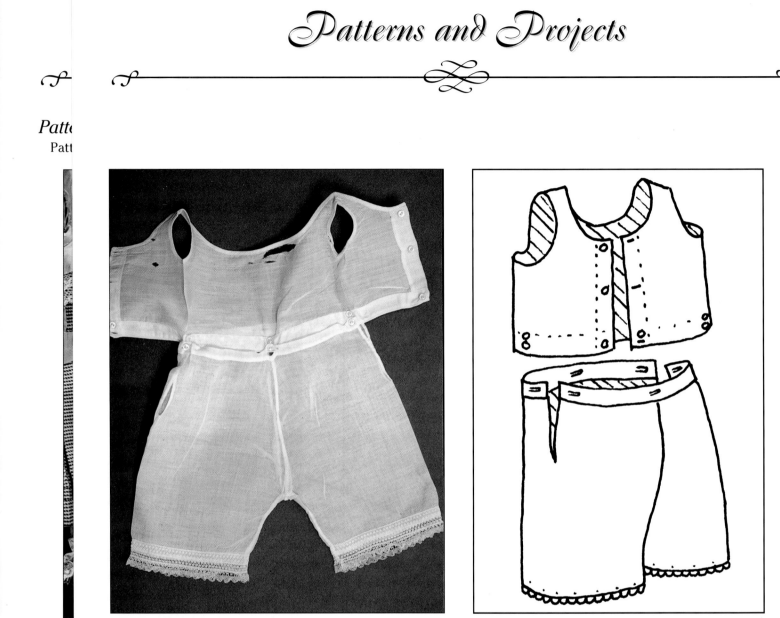

The original combination teddy from which the pattern was adapted.

Back view of two-piece combination teddy; chemise and drawers.

Pattern for Combination Teddy

Pattern adapted by Jo Ann Spencer.

Drafted and adapted from original undies worn by a French doll, this pattern should fit a 17" French doll with a 13" body.

Made of fine batiste, the teddy is machine stitched with French seams. The drawers are lace trimmed at leg bottoms, have two side openings, and button onto the bottom of the chemise with six handmade buttonholes. The chemise buttons in back with a total of ten buttons.

CHEMISE

Step 1 — Chemise: Turn under the back edges and top stitch about ½" from edges.

Step 2 — Turn under hem and top stitch about ½" from edges.

Step 3 — Face the arm holes with ⅝" bias strips.

Step 4 — Join the shoulder seams.

Step 5 — Face the entire neck edge with ⅝" bias strip.

Step 6 — Overlap the back edge and make 3 buttonholes (note placement of buttons and buttonholes). Hint: Use Fray Check to prevent ravels on fabric edges and to reinforce buttonholes.

Pattern fits a 17" French doll with 13" body

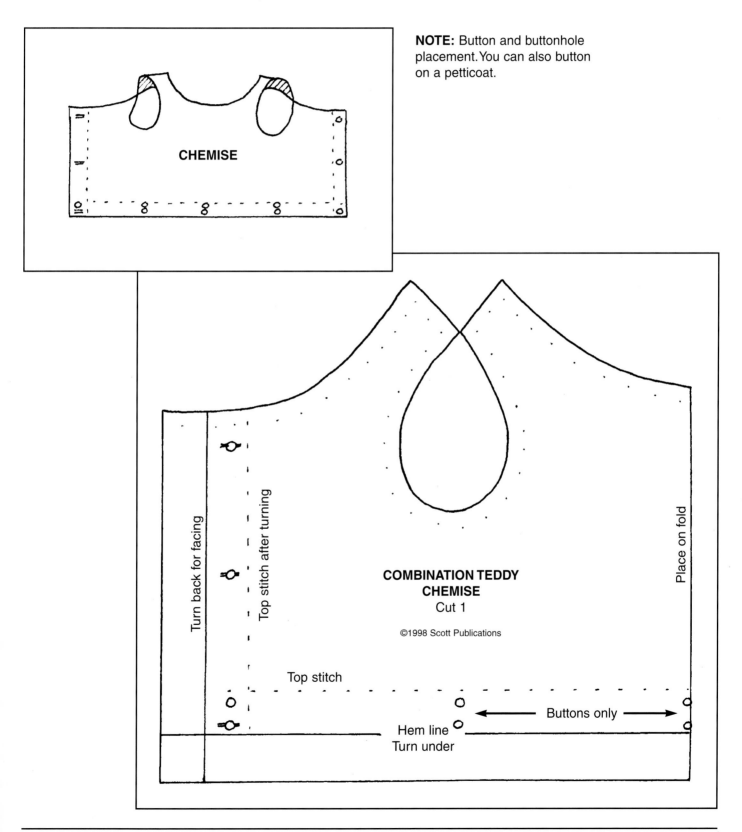

CHEMISE

NOTE: Button and buttonhole placement. You can also button on a petticoat.

Turn back for facing

Top stitch after turning

COMBINATION TEDDY CHEMISE
Cut 1

©1998 Scott Publications

Place on fold

Top stitch

Buttons only

Hem line
Turn under

Pattern for Combination Teddy, cont.'d Pattern adapted by Jo Ann Spencer.

DRAWERS
Step 1 — Hem bottom of legs; add lace.
Step 2 — Seam Center Front and Center Back, matching notches.
Step 3 — Stitch leg openings from hem to hem.
Step 4 — Clip side openings and bind with ⅝" bias strips.

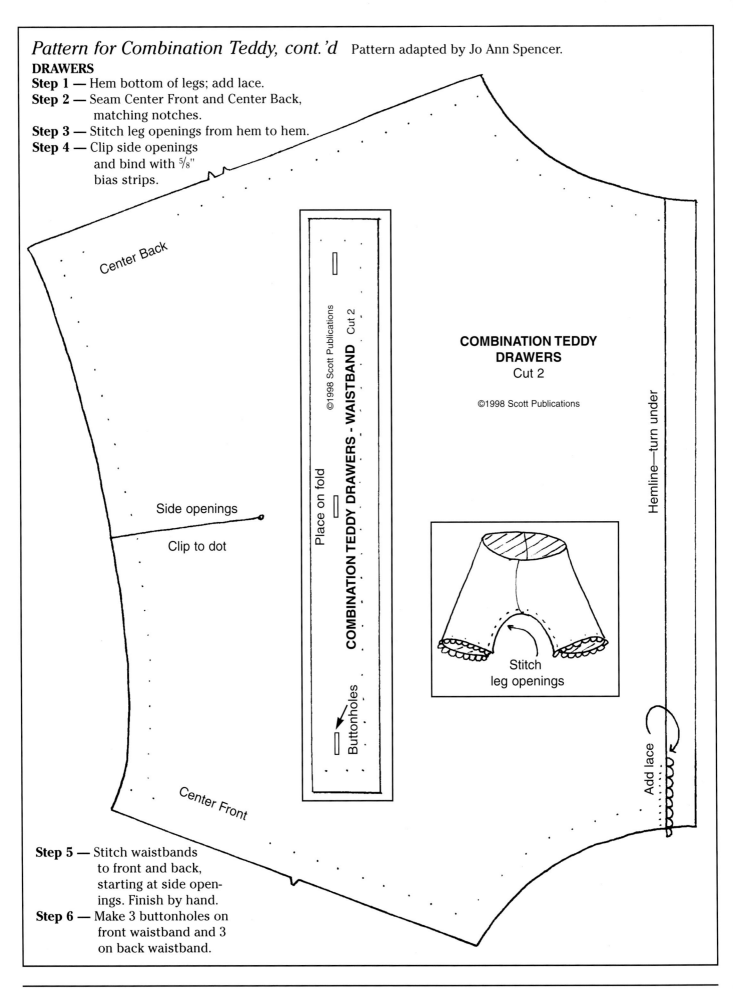

Center Back

Side openings

Clip to dot

Place on fold

©1998 Scott Publications

COMBINATION TEDDY DRAWERS - WAISTBAND Cut 2

Buttonholes

COMBINATION TEDDY DRAWERS
Cut 2

©1998 Scott Publications

Hemline—turn under

Stitch leg openings

Add lace

Center Front

Step 5 — Stitch waistbands to front and back, starting at side openings. Finish by hand.
Step 6 — Make 3 buttonholes on front waistband and 3 on back waistband.

Child's Stay to Fit a Body Circumference of 8½"-9½"

By Duby Seeley

Drawn from original antique child's stay.

The piece is lined with all edges finished, and all top stitching goes through the lining. The five-piece top and five-piece lining are cotton sateen. Please use teeny, tiny stitches. Cut one of each piece

FINISHED STRAPS

$^3/_8$" wide

Outside

Inside
unfinished ends

There are
FIVE STAYS
consisting of four rows of stitching with cord in the channels.

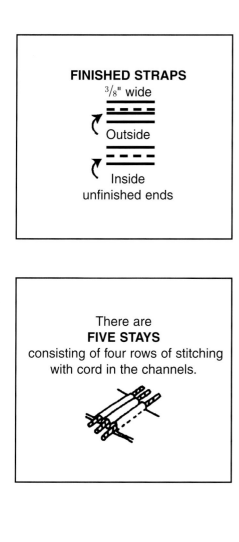

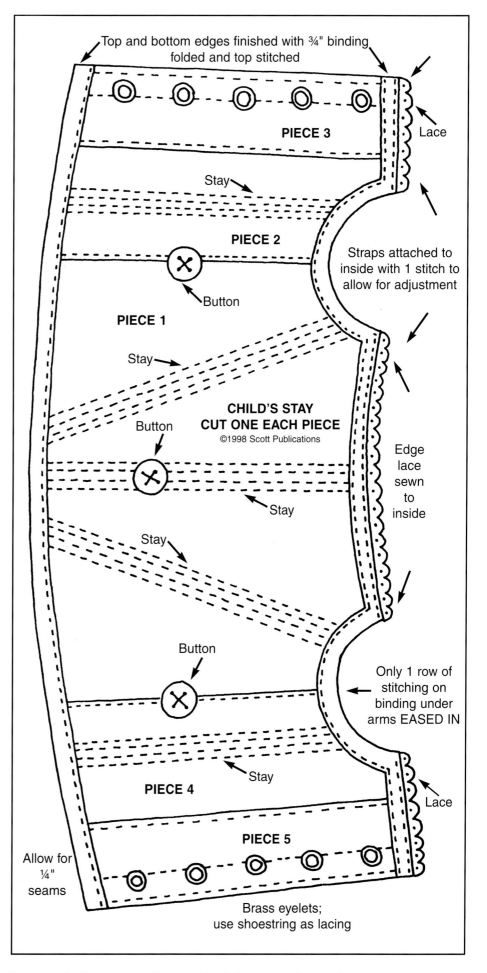

Top and bottom edges finished with ¾" binding folded and top stitched

PIECE 3

Lace

Stay

PIECE 2

Straps attached to inside with 1 stitch to allow for adjustment

Button

PIECE 1

Stay

**CHILD'S STAY
CUT ONE EACH PIECE**
©1998 Scott Publications

Button

Edge lace sewn to inside

Stay

Stay

Button

Only 1 row of stitching on binding under arms EASED IN

Stay

PIECE 4

Lace

Allow for ¼" seams

PIECE 5

Brass eyelets;
use shoestring as lacing

Conclusion to the Study

Until this study, I never realized how much handwork went into creating the dolls' white wear. Really, I hadn't appreciated all those fine seams and tiny stitches prior to such careful inspection. I found fancy decorations and handwork that was beyond belief— on dolls!

During this period, I removed clothing from dolls in my collection that had never been undressed. I "uncovered" what they did and didn't wear, and what had been lost over the years. I found dolls with other dolls' underclothes— some too big, some too small. Many were "French vanillaed" with age, some were frayed.

I found nearly all dolls had the three basic pieces of underclothing: chemise, drawers and petticoat. The real fun was discovering the special pieces, like the wire bustle on a lady doll, the hoops on a Bru, the stays on a Bru Breveté, the teddies on Jumeaux, and buttoned-on drawers and petticoats.

I found corsets on lady dolls and on Bru Bébés. I also found as many designs for chemises as there were chemises: with and without sleeves, with V-necks, round and very low necklines, with drawstrings and with buttons, lace trimmed and plain.

Petticoats came in layers. The most on one doll was four, the top one being a dust ruffle. Petticoats came mostly with a waistband or drawstring; however, a few had tops sewn to the band with buttons down the back. Usually, the petticoats were billowy, with layers of tucks, insertions and lace or eyelet on the bottom. Sometimes there was embroidery; many times it was feather stitching, crocheting or tatting.

It just didn't seem possible to me that the tiny, carefully done buttonholes could have been done by hand, but they were. Also, the smallest French seams are so perfect, with such tiny stitches, it seems impossible. I found tucks by the dozens—hand done! There even were buttons covered in matching fabrics, and insertion was used like it only took a jiffy to sew in.

I must say again, I had never truly appreciated this beautiful handwork until now. Once acknowledged, I felt it was a shame to cover up all these trims and fine needlework, so this chronicle is meant to showcase just a little– to save it.

With 50 years of dolls and ceramics, 80 years of life, 26 books, and a new doll or two, that pretty well sums it up. It is my sincere hope that everyone who reads this book will find something to like and new ideas to initiate a desire to reproduce some of the rich history that dolls provide to us.

Mildred Seeley

Above, Mildred Seeley
"I like bears, too."

14" Circle and
Dot Bru in linen
split drawers
with lace cuffs.

A 22" incised Jumeau
in her handmade
underwear, shoes
and socks.